Print Ideas

The ideas in this book were contributed by
Elisabeth and Pierre Baulig
Rita Davies
Elizabeth Holder
Alan Lewis
Mary Seyd
Roger Tingle

Evans

Evans Brothers Limited

Published by Evans Brothers Limited,
Montague House, Russell Square,
London, WC1B 5BX

Set in 12 on 13 point Photina by Filmtype Services Limited, Scarborough
and printed in Great Britain by Sackville Press Billericay Ltd, Essex

ISBN 0 237 44975 7   PRA 6576

Print Ideas

Contents

Read this first

Printing is a technique by which an image is impressed on a surface. The example with which everyone is most familiar is the printing of books and newspapers. Sophisticated machines are used to transfer an identical image (the words and pictures on a page) on to paper thousands of times. But the principles on which these machines work are essentially the same as the principles of printing described here.

The purpose of this book is to encourage you to experiment with the techniques which are described here. There are endless possibilities for printing with different materials on to different surfaces and with different inks or paints; once you have grasped the basic ideas there should be no limit to the number of ways you can use them to interpret the ideas in your imagination into finished prints. Don't think that you can't start unless you have exactly the right equipment. Experimenting and 'making do' often leads to new ways of doing things.

One thing to remember when you are planning your prints is that the image can be obtained in two ways. You can cut a design into the surface of a printing block (for example as in linoleum cuts, page 89), so that the image is not inked by the roller, does not transfer any ink to the paper and therefore appears white when the block is printed.

'Chinese Rickshaw' — a print made from a plaster block and printed in different colours.

Alternatively, you can make a design from some other material stuck on to the surface of the printing block (as for example in string blocks, page 28) so that the design itself is the only part of the block which receives ink from the roller, and therefore the only part that prints on to the paper. This is a positive image.

Paper
Any kind of paper is useful, and different surfaces produce a variety of effects.

The simplest to use is white or coloured drawing paper which is not too thick, or strong typing paper. Other papers which will take kindly to your first efforts are detail paper, layout paper, duplicating paper, tissue paper, kitchen shelf paper, and 'Jap' printing paper. Later on, when you have become really proficient, you should ask your local art shop for advice about specially prepared printing papers.

Incidentally, it is a good idea to try out your prints on newspaper first, as it is cheap and readily available.When you are satisfied with your block you can go on to print it on better paper.

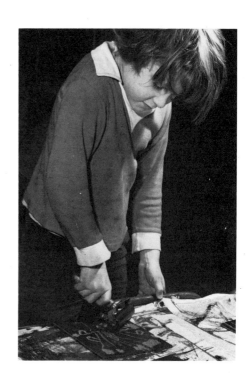

Printing inks

There are two main types of printing ink: water-based, which is soluble in water for cleaning purposes; and oil-based which is soluble in turpentine or white spirit. Both types can be obtained in tubes or pots from an art supplier. To obtain the best results, about 1cm ($\frac{1}{2}$in) should be squeezed on to the palette then spread evenly over a large area with a roller. The effect of this is to 'break down' the ink and give a finer result.

Home-made printing ink can be made by mixing one teaspoonful of powdered paint with one teaspoonful of wallpaper paste (already mixed) to make a stiff, tacky paste. Alternatively the paint can be mixed with an equal amount of Vaseline, but this is slow to dry.

For certain experiments the printing ink is

8

diluted with white spirit or turpentine (turps). These products should be handled very carefully. Never swallow any of them, or lick your fingers when working with them. Wash your hands well in hot water and soap when you have finished. Never use them near a flame — even a candle-flame — and work in a well-ventilated room with the window open, as their strong smell can give you a headache. These products evaporate in the air, so close the bottles tightly immediately after use. You can buy them in hardware and paint shops.

Paints
Use poster or powdered paints and if the paint is ready mixed do not add any more water, simply remove it from the jar with a plastic spoon and, as with printing ink, roll it out on to the palette. Household decorating paint can also be used for this.

Rollers
These are made from firm rubber, and roll over the ink or paper by means of a metal bracket and wooden handle. They usually measure between 10 to 29cms (4 to 9in) and are suitable for any type of printing. After use they should be cleaned carefully with either water or the appropriate cleaning fluid (depending on the type of ink being used) and should be stored so that there is no pressure on the rubber, which will make the roller uneven in time. If you cannot obtain a rubber roller, some hardware and household supply stores sell quite cheap metal rollers with replaceable foam plastic covers.

You will also need a surface on which to roll out the printing ink or paint. This can be a sheet of metal or a plastic tray, but the best surface is a piece of glass either square (20 × 20cm/8 × 8in) or rectangular (20 × 25cm/8 × 10in). You can buy pieces of glass like this from a hardware store or glass merchant. Make sure that the cut edges have been properly filed and polished so that they are not sharp. Glass is fragile, so handle it with care. Wash it after each experiment and you can use it again and again. If you can't get glass, use a piece of laminated wood bought from a timber yard or do-it-yourself shop.

If you don't use a roller to put ink on to your block, you can use a dye pad made

A clay block has been used to make this print: the same block was used to overprint in a lighter colour.

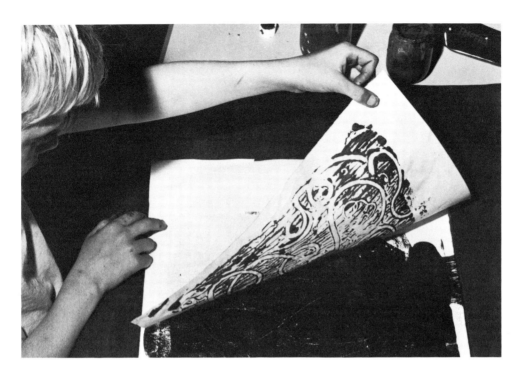

Always peel the paper carefully off your printing plate so as not to smudge the wet ink.

from a piece of foam rubber resting in a tin lid. Squeeze ink on to the rubber and press your printing block into the ink several times until it is properly charged.

Any work with paints and inks can be messy, so before you begin, cover your work table with three or four layers of newspaper and have more newspaper handy to replace it when dirty, to cover the floor if necessary, and to leave your prints on to dry. Clean rags are useful for cleaning up hands and equipment. To save your own clothes, roll up your sleeves and wear an overall or an old shirt.

Card silhouettes

Collect
Plain or coloured drawing paper (if you
have no coloured paper, you can give the
plain paper a coat of poster paint)
Printing inks or poster paints
Glass or plastic tray for a palette
An old sponge cut up into small pieces
Sheets of thin card
Plenty of old newspapers   Pencil
Brush   Drawing pins   Scissors

How to start
1. Take the newspapers and spread them
thickly on the working surfaces.
2. Pin a large piece of drawing paper on
to the newspaper.
3. Decide what shapes you are going to
use for the design (for example, animals,
birds, people, or just abstract shapes).
4. Draw the outlines on the card and cut
round the shapes.
5. Pin the shapes in position on top of the
drawing paper, using drawing pins.
6. Put several different coloured inks or
paints on your palette and, using a
different piece of sponge for each colour,
dab around the edge of the cardboard
shapes. If you have positioned the shapes
close together you will find that, besides
having the texture of the sponge, the
different colours will mix with one
another. When you remove the card
templates you will be left with a dark
(or light) silhouette and a multi-coloured
background. Paint in details.

Stencil pictures

This is the opposite process from the silhouettes described in the last idea. Here the hole left when a shape has been cut from a piece of card is used as a stencil.

Collect
Stencil brush
Knife
Pencil
Drawing paper
Stiff paper or card
Powder paint
Scissors

How to start
1. Draw a simple design on a small square of stiff paper or card.
2. Cut this out carefully so as not to break the square.
3. Place the square on the drawing paper and use the stencil brush to paint on colour inside the cut-out shape.
4. Take off the square carefully and repeat (or use another stencil) making an overall pattern on the paper.

Now experiment
Try using the shapes left in the card after you cut out the silhouette shapes for the last idea. You could make a wall frieze such as 'The Circus', 'The Jungle', or 'The Animals going into the Ark'.

A paper doily, either whole or cut up into segments, would make a good stencil too.

13

'Harbour Scene' — a card silhouette print.

Printing with junk

Collect
A large selection of odds and ends, such
as matchboxes; cardboard tubes; off-cuts
of wood; scraps of fabric with an
interesting texture, such as corduroy or
lace; corks; cotton reels; buttons or screws
Printing inks or thick poster paint
A sheet of white paper
Plasticine   Roller
A sheet of metal or glass, or a dish

How to start
1. Roll out some ink or paint on to the
glass sheet.
2. Take your scrap materials and press

14

This print was made by painting just round the edges of a stencil.

them into the paint and then on to the paper to make a pattern.

3. You will find flat objects such as buttons, coins and material easier to handle if you press them on to a lump of Plasticine first, as this acts as a handle.

Now experiment
Because of the regularity of shapes which you can achieve, this is a very good way of making a repeat pattern over a large area. Objects may be grouped together or used to suggest a definite picture.

Finger printing

Even hands and feet can be used to good effect.

Collect
Drawing paper
Plastic tray
Plenty of newspaper
Brush
Poster paint or printing ink

How to start
1. Pour the paint or ink into a flat tray or dish and dip just your finger tips into it.
2. Press them down firmly on to the drawing paper.
3. Now place the whole of the palm of the hand into the paint and make a hand print.
4. If you have ever made shadow pictures with your hands on the wall, you will know how some finger prints can look like birds or animals, or a row of soldiers

presenting arms. Try to reproduce these effects on your paper. You can add extra details by painting them in with a brush and different coloured paint.

Now experiment
Take prints of your feet in the same way, or combine hand prints and foot prints in one picture. This can be very messy, so cover the floor under and around you completely with plenty of newspaper.

Leaf printing

Collect
Printing inks or thick poster paint
A thick paint brush or roller
A sheet of glass or metal or a dish
Smooth cartridge or layout paper
A selection of leaves of different shapes and sizes. Choose ones which have well-defined veins on the underside, such as horse chestnut, ivy, rose

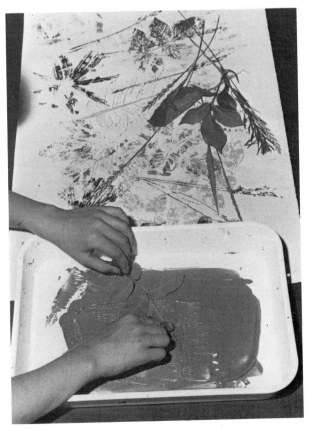

Above. Various bits of junk were used to make this fine picture of a caterpillar.

Right. The print above was made with fingers only, the one below was printed with hands and feet.

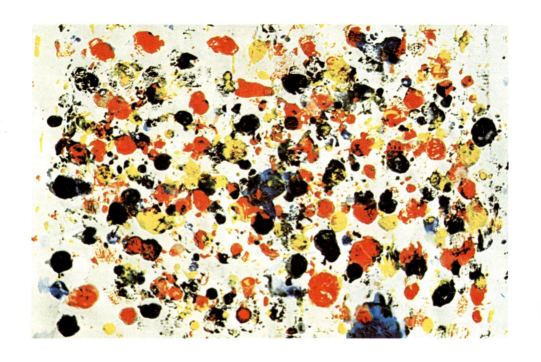

How to start
1. Spread the ink or paint with a brush
or roller on to the sheet of glass.
2. Press the leaf underside down into the
colour and then transfer it to the paper and
press it down firmly so that it almost sticks
to the paper.
3. Peel off the leaf very carefully to reveal
a detailed image.

Now experiment
Arrange the leaf prints to complete a
picture such as part of a tree, or flowers.

An interesting collection of leaf prints could
be made; you could identify each one with
the aid of a suitable reference book, and
label it with the name of the plant it
comes from.

A sheet of paper covered with prints
makes an attractive book cover.

Like leaves, feathers are ideal for printing
in fine detail, and these can be used to fill
in an outline drawing of a bird most
effectively.

Carbon paper printing

In this idea, carbon paper is used instead
of printing ink or paint to transfer the
image to the paper.

Collect
Leaves, feathers, wallpaper, etc., anything
which is thin and suitable for printing
Newspaper
Carbon paper
Roller
Drawing paper

How to start
1. Place a piece of drawing paper on to
the table in front of you.
2. On top of this put a sheet of carbon
paper, face downwards.
3. Arrange a variety of thin objects over
these two sheets of paper.
4. Cover these objects with a sheet of
newspaper and roll firmly over them two or
three times with a printing roller.
5. When the carbon paper is removed, a
print of the object is revealed underneath.

Now experiment
See what other odds and ends have an
interesting texture which could be printed
effectively by this method. You could try
string, or scraps of fabric.

String printing

Collect
Lengths of string or twine
Scissors   Drawing paper
Poster paint
Plastic tray

How to start
1. Put some paint in a flat tray or dish.

Leaves and grasses make very finely detailed, delicate prints.

2. Cut pieces of string of different lengths and dip them into the tray.
3. When they are soaked in colour lay them on your paper and twist them about.
4. Just by twisting and looping the string on the paper many different patterns can be made.

Now experiment
Try printing with different colours on the same piece of paper. Or try using different kinds of string — thick hairy string, or smoothly twisted string — to obtain different effects.

This string print has produced an effect almost like marbling.

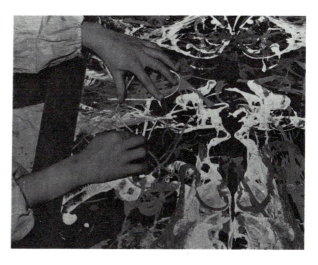

23

Printing from a card block

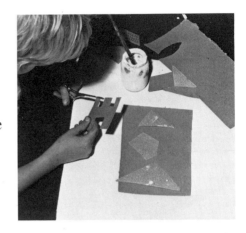

All the ideas so far have used a ready-made surface (i.e. the natural texture of an object) to print from. The next step is to create your own surfaces to print from.

Collect
Thin card (manilla board)
Pencil
Scissors
Rollers
Printing ink or poster paint
Sheet of glass for a palette
Strong glue
Drawing paper

How to start
1. Cut a square of thin card.
2. Draw some shapes on to another piece of card and cut them out.
3. Stick these shapes on to your square piece of card, and leave to dry.
4. When the block is ready, apply paint or ink with a roller and press the block firmly on to a sheet of drawing paper.

Now experiment
Try building up your block gradually and printing each time with a different colour. For example, begin with a house, stick it on the card and print it in yellow. Then add some trees, windows, doors, etc., and print again in green, and so on until a complete picture has been created.

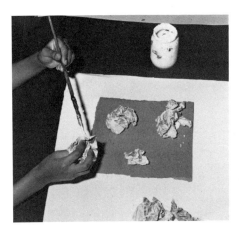

Printing from a paper block

Collect
A piece of strong card
Newspaper
Glue such as Elmer's or PVA
Roller
A piece of glass
Printing inks or thick poster paint
Drawing paper

How to start
1. Crumple up some bits of newspaper into balls of varying shapes and sizes.
2. Stick the pieces of newspaper on to the piece of card with the glue.
3. Roll out some ink or paint on to the glass sheet.
4. Press the newspaper block into the paint and print it on to the paper.

A card block was used to print the picture of huts and palm
trees above.

In the picture on the right, the stalks of the flowers were
painted in first, and the blossoms printed on afterwards, using
a paper block.

Printing with a string block

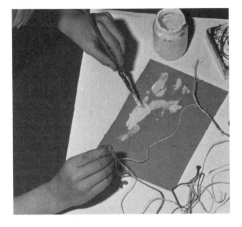

Collect
Thick card
Brush
Scissors or a sharp knife
Printing inks or poster paints
A sheet of glass
Roller
Strong glue which does not dissolve when wetted
A variety of strings and twines

How to start
1. Cut a piece of thick card for the block and brush an even coat of glue over one side.
2. Cut up the string into manageable lengths and press these into the glue.
3. As you lay the string on the block twist it, loop it, curl and knot it until you have an interesting pattern. You could fray the ends of some pieces, or plait some lengths together, or roll one length into a tight whorl.
4. When the glue has dried, roll paint or ink over the block and print it in the usual way on to drawing paper.

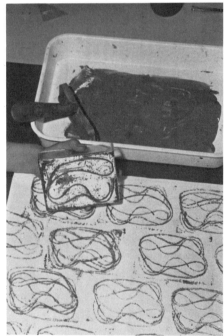

Now experiment
Overprinting can give very attractive results. Print the same pattern in two or three different colours, one over the other.

Reverse prints are fun to make. Fold the

paper in half. Open it out again, print your block on one half, and before it has dried, fold over the other half and blot it.

String prints look splendid on thin paper such as tissue paper, and this comes in beautiful rich colours. The print will show through the transparent paper to give a reverse print.

Printing in clay

This idea uses string to press patterns into clay rather than on to paper.

Collect
Lengths of string
Thick card
Strong glue
Ball of modelling clay
Paint and varnish
Cotton reels

How to start
1. Coat the card with glue, make a pattern on it with string, and allow to dry.
2. Do not make your pattern too large, as it is difficult to remove the clay if the string block is too big. For small patterns, use the end of a cotton reel instead of a piece of card to glue the string pattern on.
3. Take a small ball of clay between the palms of your hands and flatten it. Press it on to the string pattern firmly and then remove it carefully. Put the clay aside to harden, then paint and varnish it.

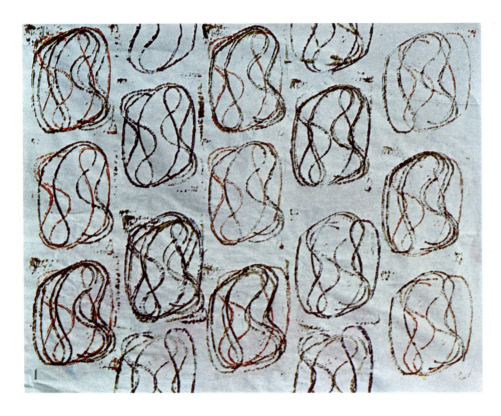

A simple string block print.

Now experiment
You can make these clay shapes into brooches and earrings, by attaching clips which you can buy at craft shops. Or pendants can be made by making a small hole through the top before the clay has dried and then threading it on a thong.

You can also use the clay shapes themselves for printing, as you can see from the next idea.

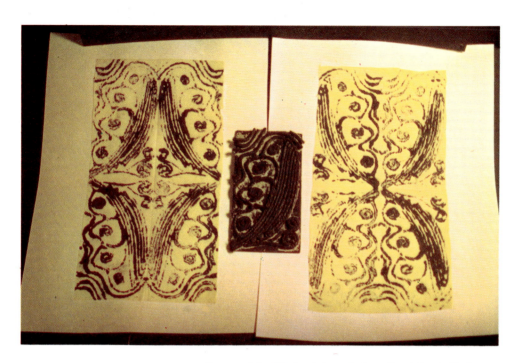

Reverse string block prints made from the elaborate block shown in the centre of the picture.

Printing with clay

Collect
Some firm modelling clay
A flat dish with a piece of sponge or cloth
on the bottom
Paper to print on (coloured, if possible)
Modelling tool
Poster paints
Newspaper

How to start
1. Take a ball of clay the size of a golf ball.
2. Gently thump it on a flat surface.
3. Use a tool or your finger to make some
marks on the flat surface of the clay.
4. Pour some paint on to the sponge in
the flat dish.
5. Press the clay block against the sponge
to pick up some colour.
6. Make a print on newspaper. Print a
pattern.
7. Wipe the clay clean with a sponge and

add to the pattern by printing in a different colour.

8. Once you are confident, make a really good print on clean paper.

Now experiment
Print a pattern in one colour and overprint in a contrasting colour.

Cut your clay blocks into shapes which fit into one another.

Use odds and ends of clay shapes to print pictures.

Printing with a piece of vegetable

Collect
A vegetable such as a potato, carrot or turnip
Printing inks or poster paints
Drawing paper
Knife   Brush

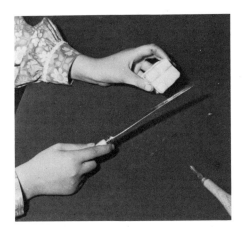

How to start
1. Cut the vegetable in half.
2. Cut a pattern across the open surface of the vegetable. Remember that the area which you have not cut will be the area which will print.
3. Dip the brush into the paint or ink and colour over the cut surface.
4. Print by pressing the piece of vegetable firmly down on to the drawing paper.
5. Make a pattern by repeating the print all over the paper.

String prints in clay.

This vegetable print was made using green ink first and overprinting with yellow ink.

Now experiment
When you have cut the surface of the vegetable but before you have printed it, try rubbing the surface with emery or glass paper. This is a kind of smooth sandpaper which will scuff the surface and should give you a better print.

If you use an apple or an onion, there is no need to cut a pattern into the surface after you have cut the fruit in half. Its natural pattern will give you an interesting print.

Printing with a plaster block

Collect

A selection of polystyrene trays (from the supermarket)
A linoleum cutter or a pair of scissors
A basin or plastic bowl
Printing ink or poster paint
A sheet of glass or metal
Plaster of Paris or wall filler (spackle)
Water
Rollers   Indian ink
Pencil   Brush
Drawing paper

How to start

1. Put 4 heaped tablespoonsful of plaster into a basin or plastic bowl and add water, one tablespoonful at a time, until a thick cream is formed.
2. Pour this into a smooth polystyrene tray and leave it to set (about 20 minutes).
3. Remove the plaster carefully and turn the block over to reveal the smoothest side.
4. Paint the smooth surface with Indian ink.
5. When it is dry, draw a picture over the ink with a pencil and then cut out the design with a knife or the end of a pair of scissors. The picture will appear white against the black surface.
6. When the block is finished, roll some ink or paint out on your glass palette and print in the usual way.

Now experiment
You can make moulds by pressing objects into the plaster while it is still wet. When dry the objects can be removed and the block charged with colour and printed.

Roller printing

Collect
Printing ink or poster paint in several colours
Rollers (preferably one for each colour to be used)
A sheet of glass, an enamel table top, a flat dish or a sheet of hardboard
Drawing paper   Brush

How to start
1. Place a little of each colour, spaced well apart, on the sheet of glass or dish, hardboard or table top.
2. Take a clean roller for each colour and roll the colours out as evenly as possible, keeping the colours separate.

'Tall Apartments' — a print made with rollers; details have
been added later with a paintbrush.

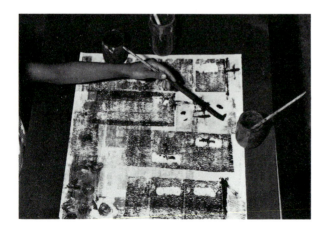

'Big Game'. Felt shapes were stuck on to a large roller to make this print.

3. Using the charged rollers, roll the different colours on to a sheet of drawing paper, making different patterns, and superimposing one colour upon another.
4. You will find that it is best to print with the darker colours first and then highlight them with the lighter colours.

Now experiment
The shapes that the rollers make may suggest a picture to you, for example, a city landscape full of sky-scrapers or Viking ships upon the sea. When you have filled your paper with roller colour, add the details with a brush and darker paint.

Felt shapes on a roller

How to start
1. With the pencil, draw in outline the pictures you would like to print on to a piece of felt. Simple shapes, such as animals, flowers or trees, are the easiest.
2. Cut out these shapes and stick them firmly on to the rolling pin or cardboard tube.
3. When the glue has dried, roll the rolling pin over the sheet of glass which has been covered with ink or paint.
4. Roll the pin over a piece of drawing paper and you will have a pattern which repeats itself as many times as you wish.

Now experiment
A complete picture can be built up in this way using different shapes. Here are some ideas for pictures: 'Noah's Ark', 'Under the Sea', 'The Zoo', 'The Farmyard', 'The Jungle'.

Collect
A rolling pin, large paint roller or cardboard tube
Printing ink or poster paint
Strong glue
Brush
Felt scraps
Scissors
Pencil
Drawing paper
A sheet of glass

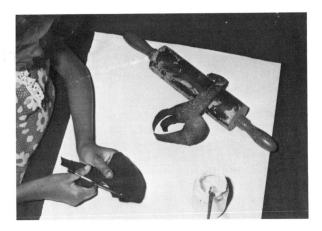

Monoprints

Monoprinting is a process of painting and printing which gives only one example of the painting or print you have made. You will see that sometimes two or three examples are taken from the same design. Nevertheless, each will be a monoprint as each is different from the rest.

The simplest monoprint is made by folding a piece of paper in two.

Smudge Prints

Collect
A sheet of cartridge or drawing paper
Poster paints in various colours
Glue
Scissors
Stiff card
String
A palette or flat dish
Brush

How to start
1. Mix some paints on the palette. They should be quite thick, yet wet enough to spread on the paper.
2. Fold the paper in half, open it and on one half, close to the centre fold, dab blobs of different coloured paints.
3. Fold the two halves of paper together again and rub over the top with your fingers to spread the paint inside.
4. Open out the paper very carefully. You will find that you have a large splodgy print with the different colours running into each other.
5. Leave the print to dry.

Now experiment
When the print is dry, cut it out and turn it into a butterfly or a many-coloured flower.

Preparing a smudge print (above) and (right) unfolding it.

*Below. Make your smudge print into a mask. Cut out the
eyes, nose and mouth, add trimmings for hair or beard, and
mount it all on a piece of stiff card. Fix string at each side of
the mask so that it can be tied round the head.*

43

Another smudge print

This technique gives a rather more delicate splattered effect.

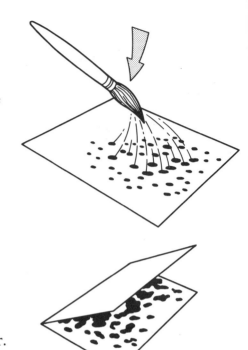

Collect
Several small containers
Powder paint or poster colours
White drawing paper
A paintbrush

How to start
1. Mix the powder paint or poster colour with a little water in a container until it is creamy.
2. Dip the brush in the paint and shake some drops of colour on to a piece of paper.
3. Fold the paper in half, pressing one half against the other.
4. Rub your hand over the fold.
5. Unfold the paper, to reveal an exciting symmetrical design.

Now experiment
Start again, using two, three, then four colours. While dripping the paint on the paper, try to plan your final result. A little green above, some brown below, and maybe your fold will give you a rare tree. Use a paintbrush and colour to outline your image.

Try using different shapes of paper and lots of different colours.

Monoprints with water colour

Collect
Powder colours
Small containers
A paintbrush or flat-ended brush
A piece of glass
White or coloured paper bigger than the
piece of glass

How to start
1. Mix the powder colours with water till
they are the consistency of runny cream.
2. Dip your brush into the paint container
and paint straight on to the glass. You
will see that the paint does not stay
exactly where you put it, and there will be
gaps where it has run back into itself,
so paint very quickly.
3. As soon as you have finished, put a
piece of paper over the design which
overlaps the glass by about 1cm ($\frac{1}{2}$in).

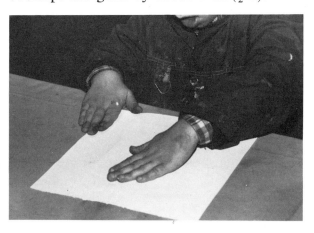

An exciting symmetrical design made by scattering paint over the paper before smudging it.

4. Press down on the paper so that it sticks to the paint and then rub it gently but firmly, being careful not to move the paper.
5. Lift off the paper carefully, starting at one corner. The design painted on the glass should be reproduced more or less exactly on the paper.

Now experiment
Wash the glass under running water (the paint will come off easily), then dry it with a rag before beginning another painting. Dip your brush in colour, and, by using

46

Bold clear colours have been used for this print made with water colours.

more or less paint, let the colours mix into each other. Take another print. By rubbing the back of the paper more or less firmly you will notice that the painting changes because the paint is less spread out in some places, or the colours have mixed in others. If you leave a large gap between the colours on the glass they will not mix in the printing.

Diluting the ink for a second print

First make a monoprint in the same way as you did for the last idea, but do not clean the glass.

Collect
The glass used for the first print
White drawing paper
A small pot of water
A paintbrush

How to start
1. When you have taken the first print from your design, wait a short time and the paint on the glass will dry. Add a few drops of water and use a wet paintbrush to spread them over the glass.
2. Lay a piece of paper over the glass and rub hard, without moving the paper.
3. Lift off the paper.
You can only take one example with this method.

Now experiment
The results you get from this method will depend on the amount of water you use; too much water, and you will get just a blurred impression on the paper, too little and you will not transfer the image at all. Once you have experimented with drops of water on the glass, try it with direct strokes of a wet paintbrush.

Finger prints with water-based ink

This paint is thick and sticky, in contrast to the paint used in the last experiment.

Collect
Water-based printing inks in tubes
(four or five different colours)
Piece of glass
Rags
Light white drawing paper bigger than the piece of glass

How to start
1. Squeeze some colour from one tube straight on to your finger and paint directly with it on to the glass.
2. Wipe your finger with a rag, choose another colour and again use your finger to paint with. Continue like this until you have finished your painting.
3. Wipe your fingers clean and place a piece of paper to overhang the glass.
4. Hold it there with one hand and with the other rub the back of the paper.
5. Carefully peel the paper off the glass, starting from one corner.
6. Leave the glass as it is, without cleaning it, for further experiments.

Now experiment
Depending on how much paint you put on first and how hard you rubbed the back of the paper, your painting will have transferred itself to the paper with more or

49

Diluting the ink with water has blended the colours in this print very effectively.

less success. Notice that the first print is almost identical to the design on the glass. You may be able to take a second print on another piece of paper. Look at it carefully; the result is quite different. If there is still ink on the glass, try a third print.

These two pictures show the difference between the first and second prints taken from the same painting on glass.

Reverse drawing on a monoprint

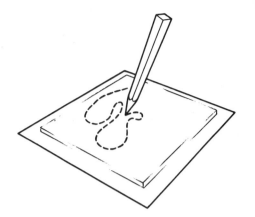

Collect
Water-based printing inks
A sheet of glass
Rollers   A pencil
A sheet of thin white drawing paper

How to start
1. Roll out some ink on to the sheet of glass.
2. Place the paper over the wet surface.
3. Draw a picture on the paper with the pencil. Take care to press gently but firmly with the pencil.
4. Peel back the paper and allow to dry.

Now experiment
Many prints can be taken from the sheet of glass without adding extra paint. Each print will vary in texture, and, unlike the first print, will have the outline of the design as a plain white line.

Try taking prints on different kinds of paper, such as tissue, crepe or cellophane.

Roll more than one colour on to the glass plate.

Using a contrasting colour on a clean glass plate, take the original monoprint (now dry), place it colour side down on to the wet surface and draw another design. Peel off and allow to dry.

Reverse drawing 2

This brings together two techniques, that of taking a monoprint from painted glass, and that of drawing on the reverse.

Collect
Water-based printing inks
Pieces of light coloured drawing paper bigger than the piece of glass
A flat brush 1cm or 2cm ($\frac{1}{2}$in or 1in) wide
A piece of sharpened wood or the handle of a paintbrush   A piece of glass

How to start
1. Paint a design on to the glass with brush and inks.
2. When the painting is finished, cover it with a piece of paper.
3. Take a piece of sharpened wood. With the pointed end, draw on the back of the paper simple upright or horizontal lines, curves etc. Make sure that the paper does not slip while you draw.
4. Lift up the paper carefully from one of the corners.
5. Wash the glass under running water and dry it with a rag.

Now experiment
The drawing you did with the piece of wood on the first print is clear and sharp but the paint becomes more and more faint as you take subsequent prints. By changing the colour of the paper and taking several prints from the original painting, you will get very different results.

Above. A street scene made by reverse drawing.

The pictures on the right show the different effects you can get from using different coloured paper for the second print. They were both taken from a painting on glass with reverse drawing.

Using black oil-based printing ink

The oil-based printing ink used in this experiment is the same as the ink used to print newspapers. It stains very easily, so make sure you have lots of newspapers on your work surface, and plenty of rags and cleaning fluid (white spirit or turps) at hand. The print you make will take a long time to dry, so have extra newspapers ready where you can leave the prints to dry out.

How to start
1. Press the ink gently out of the tube straight on to the brush.
2. Paint on to the glass. Take more ink as you need it to finish the design.
3. When the painting is ready, take a print.
4. Clean the glass and your brush immediately with a piece of rag soaked in white spirit. When you have removed all

Collect
A tube of black printing or typographic ink
A flat brush about 1cm ($\frac{1}{2}$in) wide
A piece of glass
Rags
Several pieces of white drawing paper
A glass pot filled with white spirit

the ink from the glass plate, wipe it
completely clean with a dry rag.

Now experiment
Take several prints. Dry your examples
between single pages of a newspaper —
without piling them up — because they will
need three to eight days to dry out
completely.

Using coloured oil-based printing ink

Printing inks come in other colours besides
black. If you have tubes of ink in the
primary colours, red, blue and yellow, and
a tube of white, you can mix any other
colour you want.

Collect
Two glass plates
One or two flat brushes of different widths
White or coloured paper
Four tubes of printing ink — white, red,
blue, yellow
A palette knife
Rags
A small glass pot of white spirit

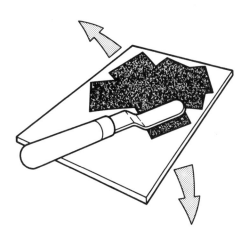

How to start
1. Mix together the colours you are going
to use with a little white spirit and the
palette knife on one glass plate.
2. Use the brushes to paint a design on the
other glass plate. Place a piece of white
paper on that glass.

Use black oil-based ink for bold designs like this one of a bird.

3. Rub the back of the paper and lift it off gently, beginning from one corner.

Now experiment
Try various colours, mixing the inks in different proportions. You could try mixing half red and half yellow, or one-third blue and two-thirds yellow. Try mixing the colours irregularly, to produce unexpected results. Experiment with the warm colours — reds, yellows, oranges, browns and some purples — and with the cold — blues, greens and other purples. Try white ink alone on a coloured background for a dramatic result.

Above. White ink only, on coloured paper, was used for this picture of a snail.

Below. A bird, printed with several coloured inks on to white paper.

A second print with white spirit

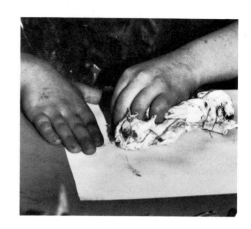

Before you clean a glass plate that you have used for oil-based inks and have taken several prints from, experiment by using left-over materials.

Collect
A glass plate coated with printing ink which has already been used
Some sheets of thin white paper
A rag
A small glass pot of white spirit
Some clean brown wrapping paper

How to start
1. Rest the piece of paper for your print on a good backing of wrapping paper. Rub over the sheet gently with a rag dipped in white spirit.
2. Lay this piece of paper on the used plate and rub over it with the rag soaked in white spirit.
3. Remove the paper from the plate and if there is any colour left on the plate immediately place another piece of paper over it and rub.

Now experiment
You will see that the end product from this experiment has nothing to do with your original print. You will get yet another result if you take a second print with a sheet of coloured paper which is thin enough for the white spirit to soak through.

Roller and rag

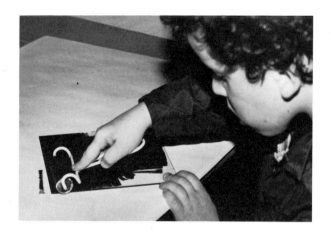

Collect
A small printing roller about 10cm (4in) long
A tube of black or coloured printing ink
A glass plate
A dry rag
A pointed stick or the handle of a paintbrush
White and coloured paper
White spirit

How to start
1. Put a little ink on the glass and use the roller to spread it evenly over the entire surface.
2. Use the dry rag to wipe away the ink from the places where your design will be.
3. Take a print as usual. You will notice that the design is made from the parts where you have used the rag to take off the ink, making a negative picture.

Now experiment
Try out other effects using points (ends of sharpened wood, a nail, rolled-up paper,

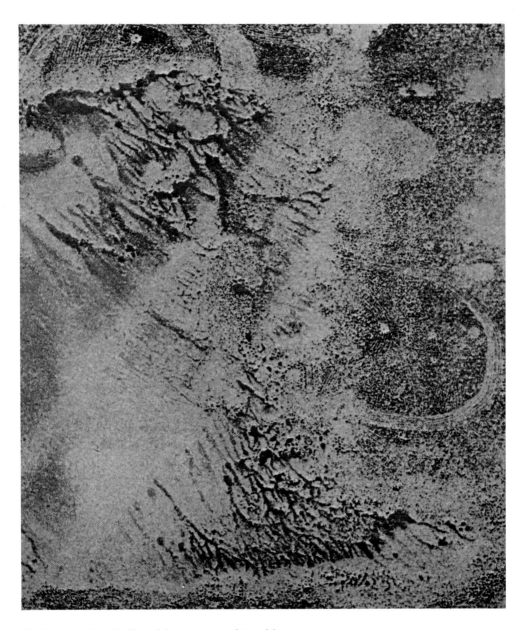

*The dramatic blurred effect of this print was obtained by
taking a second print with white spirit.*

Use bold strokes of your finger with the rag wrapped round it to remove the ink from the plate before taking a print.

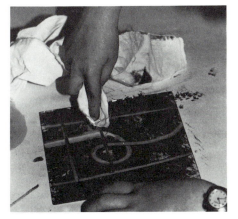

in fact anything which will scratch the ink from the glass plate).

Don't rub too hard on the back of the paper, or you will spoil the picture underneath. You will get different results according to how thickly you spread your ink on the plate and how uniformly the roller picks it up.

Wet rag on a one-colour background

This time, instead of using a dry rag, use a rag dipped in a mixture of white spirit and black printing ink, and ink the glass with a coloured printing ink.

Collect
Two tubes of printing ink – one black and one coloured
An ink roller
A glass plate
White paper
Rags   White spirit
A small glass pot

How to start
1. Cover the entire surface of the glass with coloured printing ink, using the roller. Spread it well without making it too thick.
2. In a small glass pot mix a little black printing ink with white spirit and dip in the rag.
3. Draw on the inked plate with the rag. You will be removing the coloured ink and leaving a little black ink at the same time.
4. Lay a sheet of white paper over the plate and rub hard.
5. Lift up the piece of paper. The bits removed by the rag will come out in white outlined in black.

Now experiment
This technique is particularly effective for autumn landscapes or foggy scenes.

64

Using diluted printing ink

Wash is a technique which uses Indian ink or a colour diluted with water to make a picture. This idea shows how to get the same effect with printing inks. Take care — these inks are very thick and oily and should be diluted with white spirit or turps, but never with water.

Collect
Several glass pots to hold different coloured washes   A glass plate   Rags
Coloured printing inks
A bottle of turps or white spirit
Flat and round brushes
White and coloured paper

How to start
1. Mix a little printing ink with some solvent — turps or white spirit — in each glass pot. The more solvent you use, the lighter the colour. Stir the mixture with a brush until well mixed.
2. When all your washes are ready, paint a design on a piece of glass.
3. Place a piece of paper lightly over it and press down carefully with your hand.
4. Remove the paper carefully. Nothing will remain on the glass, so you can only take one print from each painting with this method.

Now experiment
Your result will be subtle and blurred or strong with hazy outlines, depending on how much solvent you have used.

You can see from this picture of a horse how your design is outlined in black when you draw with a rag dipped in diluted printing ink.

Diluted printing ink was used to create this print of an owl.

The lighter the wash (i.e. the more diluted), the quicker the final print will dry. Experiment using washes of different colours.

White spirit and washing-up liquid

When printing ink is diluted not only with white spirit but also with washing-up liquid, it will spread unevenly over the plate. Since the washing-up liquid stops the ink spreading normally, you will get an irregular effect within the painted design.

Collect
A glass plate
Small glass pots
White drawing paper
Rags
Brushes and paintbrushes
Coloured printing inks
White spirit   Washing-up liquid

How to start
1. Mix some ink and spirit in each pot. The mixture should not be too thin – more like pancake batter.
2. Add a little washing-up liquid. Mix together until creamy.
3. Use the mixture to paint the glass.
4. Lay a sheet of paper down and rub gently without pressing.
5. You can take a second print if there is still enough paint on the glass plate.

Now experiment
Vary the grainy effect of the painting according to how much washing-up liquid you use; the more liquid, the bigger the bubbles. They will form on the surface and

can be emphasised even more if you add a little water to them.

Using Indian ink 1

Indian inks are strong and cannot be washed out, but can be diluted with water. Look at some Japanese paintings to see the graceful effect you get from 'wash'.

Collect
A glass plate
White paper
Indian inks in tubes (black and coloured)
An ordinary paintbrush and a special brush for wash

How to start
1. Using the ink straight from the tube, draw on to the glass plate with a brush.
2. Lay down a piece of paper over the glass and rub very lightly over the back.
3. Lift off the paper.

Now experiment
You will notice that the inks tend to gather in small drops on the glass so it is very difficult to get an exact outline. If you use more than one colour you will find that they mix at random giving endless different results.

Using Indian ink 2

Collect
A glass plate
White paper
Indian inks in tubes (black and coloured)
Washing-up liquid
Small glass pots
Brushes

How to start
1. Mix a little of each coloured Indian ink

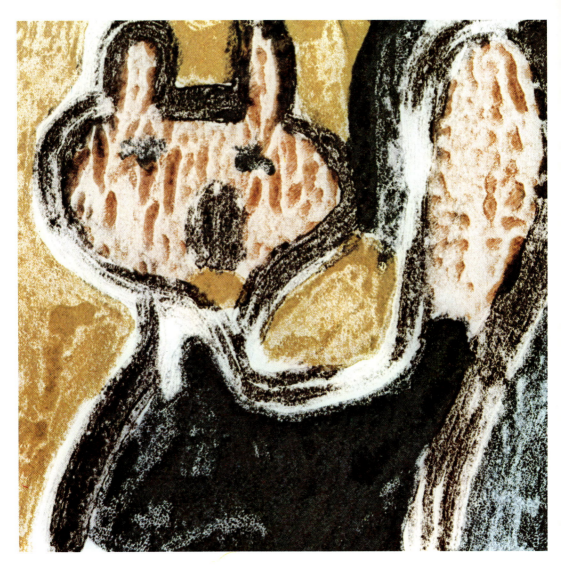

in the glass pots with some washing-up liquid until the mixture is foamy.
2. Paint a design on the glass with the mixture.
3. Place the paper down gently over the glass and rub.
4. Lift off carefully.

This fox shows the grainy effect you get from using washing-up liquid and white spirit to dilute the ink.

70

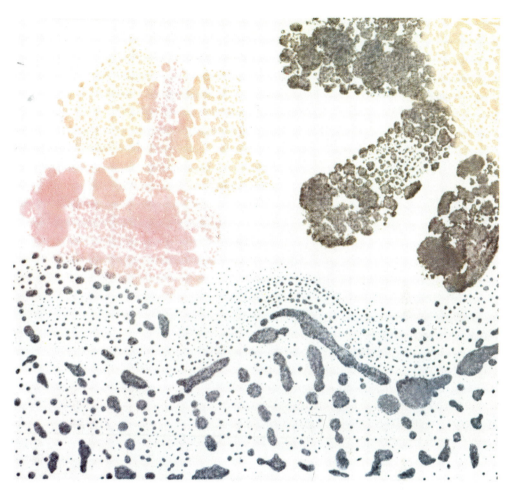

This picture shows the bubbly effect produced by diluting Indian ink with washing-up liquid.

Now experiment
By adding washing-up liquid to Indian ink you get a foam that holds the glass, so you can plan a more precise painting than that described in the last experiment. The little bubbles in the foam give a very pleasing effect. The lighter the foam, the more subtle the result.

Using oil pastels

How to start

1. Clean the glass with a clean rag soaked in turps. Dry it well with a dry rag.
2. Draw a pattern directly on to the glass with the oil pastels. Go over the lines several times to get the colours on thickly.
3. Place the paper over the glass and rub hard on the back with a rag soaked in turps. Work fast or the colours will mix.
4. Lift the paper gently to get your print.
5. You can take a second print by quickly putting another piece of paper on the glass and rubbing it with a dry cloth.

Collect
Oil pastels
Rags
White paper
Turps
A piece of glass

Now experiment

You can get more varied prints by spraying the turps over the design. Dip an old toothbrush in turps and scrape a knife over the bristles so that a fine spray of turps is scattered over the glass. Then place the paper over the glass and rub the back with a dry rag.

Another oil pastels idea

How to start

1. Dip the oil pastel into the turps.
2. Draw on to the glass using the pastel in small guide circles over your design. Make sure the pastel is leaving a mark — dip it often into the turps.
3. Place a piece of paper over the drawing and rub the back for a few seconds with your hand. Carefully peel off your print.

Collect
Oil pastels
A piece of glass
White paper
A small glass jar for turps

72

Now experiment
You have just made a faint but pleasant print. The more you go over the glass with the pastel, the clearer your colour will be. Leave a little space between colours and don't mix them by putting one on top of another because, with the addition of turps, they will no longer be transparent.

Marbling

The technique of marbling produces marvellous swirling patterns like the grain of polished marble. Although the technique is different from those already described, the results are still monoprints, as no two patterns are ever the same.

Collect
Small bottles of different coloured oil-based inks such as Lin marbling inks
A bowl of water   Vinegar
Small sheets of cartridge paper
Newspaper

How to start
1. Cover a table with newspaper for your finished patterns.
2. Carefully drip some ink colours on to the water in the bowl.
3. Add a sprinkle of vinegar to help break up the oil colours.
4. Gently swirl your finger around in the water to move and merge the inks.
5. Holding two corners of a sheet of paper, pull it through the water so that it picks up the oily colours.

These two pictures show two effects you can get using oil
pastels. The boat on the left was drawn directly on to the
glass plate with oil pastels and transferred to the paper by
rubbing with turps. The fish above was drawn with an oil
pastel dipped in turps. You can see that the colours are much
softer with the second method, and bolder and more glowing
with the method used for the boat print.

Now experiment

Instead of pulling the paper through the water, cut a piece the size of the bowl and gently rest it on the top. Lift the paper carefully so that the ink pattern is on one side only.

If you cannot get any oil-based inks, try this method using oil paints.

Sprinklings of powder paint also give an unusual result. You will not need vinegar for this method.

Marbled papers are sometimes used for the bindings and endpapers of fine and rare books. You may be able to see examples of these in museums or antiquarian bookshops, and get new ideas for colour combinations or patterns, or for using your marbled paper.

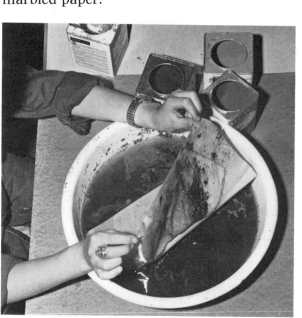

Printing on fabric

Dyes
There are two kinds of paint-dye. One is oil-based and comes in tubes. The colour of this kind does not need to be fixed. The other is water-based and comes in pots. When it is dry the colour must be fixed by ironing with a hot iron on the back of the material for about five minutes.

Equipment used with the oil-based dye needs to be cleaned with turpentine while that used with the water-based colour can be washed in water.

There are other fabric dyes which come in liquid form and instructions for their use and method of fixing should be followed.

Dye pad
A dye pad is essential for some kinds of fabric printing. Make it from a piece of wood covered with two layers of a piece of old blanket or foam rubber. Cover the whole pad with a sheet of polythene fastening it to the back of the pad with sticky tape. The dye is spread on the pad with a roller. Rollers can be bought in different sizes from an art supply store.

Printing on fabric is made easier if the material to be printed is stretched over a board. A pad of newspaper between the fabric and the board will give a flat, firm surface. Always wash and dry the fabric before printing.

Three examples of marbling. You can also print fabric with marbling techniques by diluting oil fabric dye with a little turpentine and dropping it into water. Swirl the water, then float a piece of dry material on top and draw it across the water as you lift it out. Iron the back of the fabric to fix the dye.

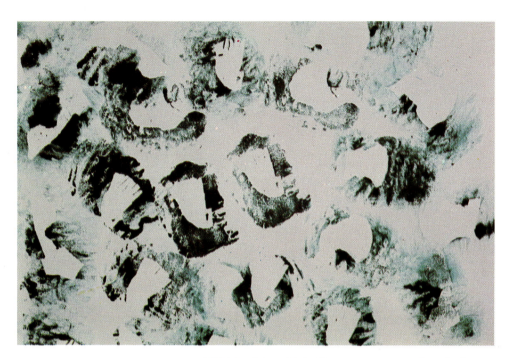

A blotch print on fabric. You can use any number of colours for your print.

Blotch printing

Collect
A piece of fabric stretched on a board
A loofah or coarse sponge
Stiff paper
Scissors   Dye pad
Paint roller
Water-based dye-paint

How to start
1. Cut the stiff paper into a pattern shape
and lay it on the material.
2. Spread the dye evenly on the dye pad
with the roller.
3. Dip the cut end or side of the loofah
into the dye and print over and around the
paper shape.
4. Place the paper shape on a different
part of the material and repeat the printing.
Do this all over the fabric. The part covered
by the paper shape will be uncoloured.
5. Dry and fix the colour with an iron.
Clean your equipment.

Now experiment

A coarse sponge can be used instead of a loofah. If three pieces of sponge are used three colours can be printed on the fabric.

Printing with templates

A template may be either a shaped hole to paint through or a solid shape to paint round.

Collect

Fabric stretched on a board
A chocolate box divider
Stiff paint brushes
Saucers
Scissors
Turps
Oil paint-dye (Water-based dye may be used but it will need fixing)

How to start

1. Cut out the bottoms of the shapes in the chocolate box divider.
2. Put small amounts of different coloured dyes into separate saucers. Use a different brush for each colour.
3. Paint through the template on to the fabric, arranging the pattern and colours as you wish.
4. Allow the dye to dry.

Now experiment

Cut out shapes from gummed paper and stick them on the fabric in a pattern. Paint over them with oil dye, using several colours. When all the fabric is coloured and the dye is dry, remove the templates.

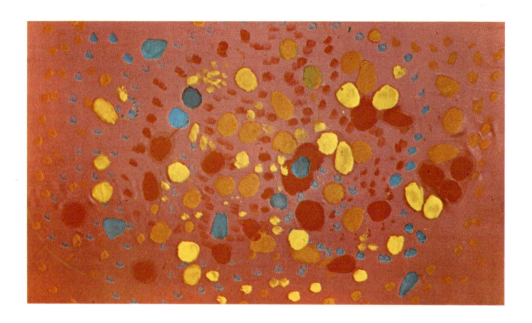

This exciting print was made using the holes in a chocolate box divider. Remember to use a separate brush, and a separate hole in the template for each colour of dye that you use so that the colours remain clear and distinct.

Templates cut from stiff card were used to make this print.

Block printing

Collect
White cotton fabric stretched on a board
Scissors   Paint roller
Fabric glue, PVA or Elmer's
Wooden mallet
Piece of wood about 8cm (3in) square and
2cm (1in) thick
Felt   Dye pad
Water-based paint-dye

How to start
1. Cut the felt into a shape which will
print on the fabric. Glue it to the wood.
2. With the roller spread a small amount
of dye evenly on the dye pad.
3. Charge the block by dabbing it on the
dye pad until the felt shape is well covered
with the dye.
4. Place the block on the material where
it is to be printed and strike it once with
the mallet or with the side of your fist.
This will print the pattern on to the fabric.
5. Continue printing. Charge the block
with dye between prints.
6. Fix the dye after it has dried by ironing
the fabric between newspaper.

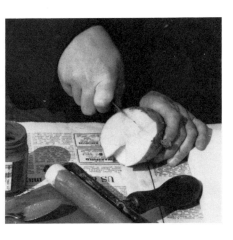

Potato printing

Cut a large potato in half and carve a shape out of the flat surface with a penknife.

Spread the dye evenly on the dye pad as before and press the potato gently on the pad to pick up the dye on the cut surface.

Using the potato as a block, print the pattern on to the material.

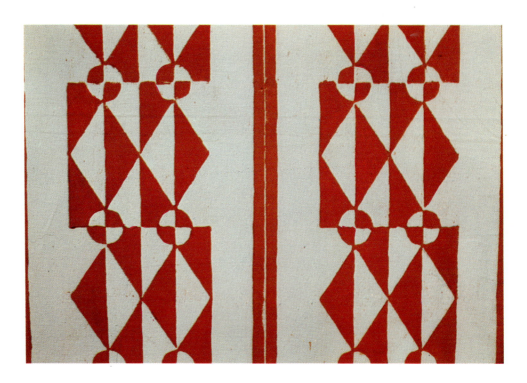

This formal border pattern was made by printing a block one way and then the other way several times. You will have to place the block very carefully so that the second print fits up exactly to the first one and so on.

A print made from a roller with pins and string on the surface. Placing the pins and string at random has produced this pleasing abstract pattern. You could also make a symmetrical pattern on the roller to produce a more formal print.

Roller printing on fabric

This experiment uses a technique described earlier in this book — making patterns on the surface of a large roller and printing from them. Here we use this technique to print continuous patterns on fabric.

Collect
Fabric stretched on a board
Roller made from a cardboard tube
Dye pad
Paint-dye
Paint roller
String
Drawing pins or thumb tacks

How to start
1. Wind some string round the roller, keeping it in place with the pins. It should be tied quite firmly.
2. Spread a little paint-dye on to the dye pad and charge the pad with dye by rolling it out with the paint roller.
3. When the dye is rolled out evenly, roll the string roller across the dye.
4. Then roll it across the fabric. The pins and string will make a continuous pattern over the fabric.
5. When the dye starts to run out return the roller to the dye pad and re-charge it with colour.

Now experiment
The pins and string can be set in a random pattern or symmetrically. Use different kinds of string to print different textures.

Pieces of felt can be stuck to the roller to make the kind of patterns shown on page 39.

Linoleum printing

Linoleum cutting is quite difficult and has many stages. It is well worth persevering until you master each step.

Collect
Linoleum cutting tools – these should include a selection of blades and a handle
Linoleum
Tray or a piece of glass
Paint roller and printing inks
Good quality drawing paper
Felt tip pen

How to start
1. Begin with a bold and simple design. Draw the outline with a felt pen on to the linoleum.
2. Before you start to cut the linoleum

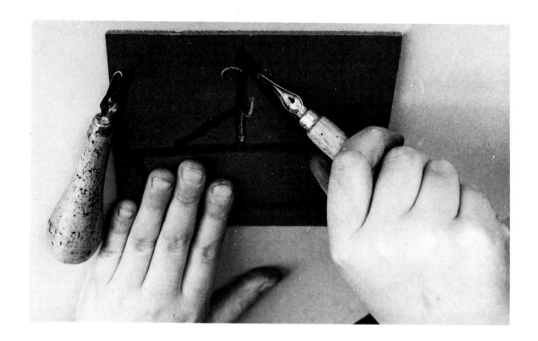

make sure that you are holding the tool correctly. Both sets of fingers must be behind the cutting edge and all the cutting must be away from your body.

Notice how to hold the cutting tool with your fingers always behind the blade. Different blades will give you deep or shallow or broad or narrow cuts.

3. Start cutting with a V-shaped cutter making an even groove along the edge of the design.

4. Squeeze some ink on to a tray or piece of glass and roll it out. Now ink the linoleum by rolling the colour on to it.

5. Place the linoleum ink-side down, on the top corner of the paper. Press it down with a clean roller to get a good print.

6. Repeat this print a number of times. Remember to ink the block again after each print.

7. Wash the linoleum and the roller clean and then make further cuts in the linoleum to add to your design. Mark the back of the

A series of lino prints in three colours — yellow, blue and red.

Rolling out the ink.

Inking the block.

linoleum with an arrow to show the top.
8. Go back to stage 4, but this time use
a different coloured printing ink. Place the
block as carefully as possible over the first
print and press it down with a clean roller.
9. When you remove the block you will see
some of the original colour as well as an
overprint of the second colour.
10. Clean the linoleum and roller again,
and then cut some more of the design
away, this time, perhaps, cutting away the
background. Print the block using a third
colour.

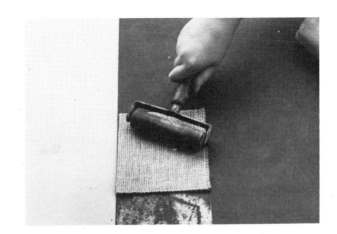

Use a roller to make sure the block comes
closely into contact with the paper.

Remove the block to reveal the print.

More details have been cut into the block for
the second printing.

Now experiment
There are hundreds of different ways you
can experiment with linoleum cuts and as
you practise and get better you will be able
to think of ideas of your own.

'Fishes in the River.'

94